One-Pot Vegan Cookbook: Fam Soup, Casserole, Slow Cooker a for Busy People on a

by Alissa Noel Grey

Text copyright(c)2016 Alissa Noel Grey

All rights reserved. No part of this publication may be reproduced, distributed, or transmitted in any form or by any means, including photocopying, recording, or other electronic or mechanical methods, without the prior written permission of the publisher, except in the case of brief quotations embodied in critical reviews and certain other noncommercial uses permitted by copyright law

Although every precaution has been taken to verify the accuracy of the information contained herein, the author and publisher assume no responsibility for any errors or omissions. No liability is assumed for damages that may result from the use of information contained within.

Table Of Contents

Delicious One-Pot Vegan Meals to Please Everyone	5
Leek, Brown Rice and Potato Soup	6
Easy Vegetable Soup	7
Curried Parsnip Soup	8
Mediterranean Chickpea Soup	9
Carrot, Sweet Potato and Chickpea Soup	10
Sweet Potato and Coconut Soup	11
Creamy Tomato and Roasted Pepper Soup	12
Fresh Asparagus Soup	13
Shredded Cabbage Soup	14
Creamy Red Lentil Soup	15
Creamy Broccoli and Potato Soup	16
Creamy Brussels Sprout Soup	17
Creamy Potato Soup	18
Lentil, Barley and Kale Soup	19
Mediterranean Lentil Soup	20
Borscht	21
Celery, Apple and Carrot Soup	22
Pea, Dill and Rice Soup	23
Minted Pea and Nettle Soup	24
Bean and Spinach Soup	25
Italian Minestrone	26
French Vegetable Soup	27
Spiced Beet and Carrot Soup	28
Cauliflower Soup	29
Pumpkin and Bell Pepper Soup	30
Wild Mushroom Soup	31
Mushroom and Kale Soup	32
Spinach and Pasta Soup	33
Lemon Artichoke Soup	34
Quinoa, Sweet Potato and Tomato Soup	35
Leek and Quinoa Soup	37
Red Lentil and Quinoa Soup	38
Spinach and Quinoa Soup	39
Vegetable Quinoa Soup	40

Tomato and Quinoa Soup	41
Kale, Leek and Quinoa Soup	42
Potato, Pea and Cauliflower Curry	43
Cauliflower with Chilli and Mustard	45
Baked Cauliflower	46
Maple Roast Parsnip with Pear and Sage	47
Balsamic Roasted Carrots and Baby Onions	48
Potato and Zucchini Bake	49
One-Pot Vegan Pizza	50
One-Pot Vegan Pasta	52
Easy One-Pot Spaghetti	53
Lentil and Olive Spaghetti	54
Summer Zucchini Risotto	55
Vegetable Quinoa Stew	56
Eggplant and Quinoa Stew	57
Comforting Quinoa Shepherd's Stew	59
Easy Moroccan Vegetable Stew with Quinoa	61
Zucchini and Buckwheat Stew	63
Power Buckwheat Stew	64
Quick Buckwheat Chilli	65
Ratatouille	66
Okra and Tomato Casserole	67
Spicy Chickpea and Spinach Stew	68
Moroccan Chickpea Stew	69
Chickpea, Rice and Mushroom Stew	71
Easy Chickpea Dinner	72
Baked Bean and Rice Casserole	73
Green Pea and Rice Casserole	74
Easy Green Bean Stew	75
Green Beans and Potatoes	76
Cabbage and Rice Stew	77
Hearty Slow Cooker Baked Beans	78
Slow Cooker Stuffed Bell Peppers	79
FREE BONUS RECIPES: 25 Superfood Paleo and Vegan Smoothies for Vibrant Health and Easy Weight Loss	80
Kale and Kiwi Smoothie	81

Delicious Broccoli Smoothie	82
Papaya Smoothie	83
Beet and Papaya Smoothie	84
Lean Green Smoothie	85
Easy Antioxidant Smoothie	86
Healthy Purple Smoothie	87
Mom's Favorite Kale Smoothie	88
Creamy Green Smoothie	89
Strawberry and Arugula Smoothie	90
Emma's Amazing Smoothie	91
Good-To-Go Morning Smoothie	92
Endless Energy Smoothie	93
High-fibre Fruit Smoothie	94
Nutritious Green Smoothie	95
Apricot, Strawberry and Banana Smoothie	96
Spinach and Green Apple Smoothie	97
Superfood Blueberry Smoothie	98
Zucchini and Blueberry Smoothie	99
Tropical Spinach Smoothie	100
Dark Green Veggie Smoothie	101
Kale and Raspberry Smoothie	102
Delicious Kale Smoothie	103
Healthy Apricot Smoothie	104
Cherry Smoothie	105
About the Author	106

Delicious One-Pot Vegan Meals to Please Everyone

One pan, pot, skillet, or slow-cooker is all you need to prepare these no-fuss vegan family dinners. For a hearty meal that requires minimal clean-up, one-pot recipes are perfect for weeknight suppers.

And while it may seem time consuming to prepare real food at home, you will soon discover that you can cook a balanced, nutritious one-pot dinner in the same amount of time you'd need to order a takeout.

From soups and stews, to simple casseroles and one-pot pasta dishes, all you need to do is simply prepare your favorite vegetables, legumes or grains, throw them together with some superfood herbs and spices in a single pot, skillet or slow cooker and relax until it's time to serve-it doesn't get easier than that!

At the end of a busy day a heartwarming one-pot dinner is a simple meal that comes together quickly and makes everyone happy. And the quick clean-up makes these recipes even more enticing!

Leek, Brown Rice and Potato Soup

Serves: 4-5

Prep time: 35 min

Ingredients:

3 potatoes, peeled and diced

2 leeks, finely chopped

1/4 cup brown rice

5 cups water

3 tbsp extra virgin olive oil

lemon juice, to taste

Directions:

Heat olive oil in a deep soup pot and sauté leeks for 3-4 minutes. Add in potatoes and cook for a minute more.

Stir in water, bring to a boil, and add the brown rice. Reduce heat and simmer for 30 minutes.

Add lemon juice, to taste, and serve.

Easy Vegetable Soup

Serves: 4-5

Prep time: 35 min

Ingredients:

2 leeks, white parts only, well rinsed and thinly sliced

1 carrot, chopped

1 cup Brussels sprouts, halved

1 potato, peeled and diced

1 garlic clove, chopped

1 red pepper, chopped

1 yellow pepper, chopped

1 cup white mushrooms, halved

4 cups vegetable broth

3 tbsp extra virgin olive oil

salt and black pepper, to taste

Directions:

Heat the olive oil in a large soup pot. Add in the leeks and cook over low heat for 2-3 minutes. Add in the Brussels sprouts, carrot, garlic, peppers and potato and cook for about 5 minutes, stirring.

Add the vegetable broth and the mushrooms and bring to a boil.

Reduce heat and simmer, uncovered, for 30 minutes, or until the vegetables are tender but still holding their shape.

Season with salt and pepper to taste and serve.

Curried Parsnip Soup

Serves: 4-5

Prep time: 40 min

Ingredients:

1.5 lb parsnips, peeled, chopped

1 onion, chopped

2 garlic cloves, chopped

2 tbsp extra virgin olive oil

1 tbs curry powder

1/2 cup coconut milk

salt and black pepper, to taste

Directions:

In a deep saucepan, gently sauté the onion and garlic together with the curry powder. Add in the parsnips and sauté, stirring often, for 5-6 minutes.

Add 4 cups of water, bring to a boil, and simmer for 30 minutes or until the parsnips are tender.

Set aside to cool then blend in batches until smooth. Return soup to the pan, stir in the milk and heat through. Season with salt and pepper to taste.

Mediterranean Chickpea Soup

Serves 4-5

Ingredients:

1 can (15 oz) chickpeas, drained

1 small onion, chopped

2 garlic cloves, minced

1 can (15 oz) tomatoes, diced

2 cups water

2 cups coconut milk

3 tbsp extra virgin olive oil

2 bay leaves

1/2 tsp dried oregano

Directions:

Heat olive oil in a deep soup pot and sauté onion and garlic for 1-2 minutes. Add in water, chickpeas, tomatoes, bay leaves, and oregano.

Bring the soup to a boil then reduce heat and simmer for 20 minutes. Add in coconut milk and cook for 1-2 minutes more.

Set aside to cool, discard the bay leaves and blend until smooth.

Carrot, Sweet Potato and Chickpea Soup

Serves: 5-6

Prep time: 35 min

Ingredients:

3 large carrots, chopped

1/2 onion, chopped

1 can (15 oz) chickpeas, undrained

2 sweet potatoes, peeled and diced

4 cups vegetable broth

2 tbsp extra virgin olive oil

1 tsp cumin

1 tsp ginger

Directions:

Heat olive oil in a large saucepan over medium heat. Add onion and carrots and sauté until tender. Add in broth, chickpeas, sweet potato and seasonings.

Bring to a boil then reduce heat and simmer, covered, for 30 minutes.

Blend soup until smooth, add in coconut milk and cook for 2-3 minutes until heated through.

Sweet Potato and Coconut Soup

Serves: 4-5

Prep time: 35 min

Ingredients:

1 small onion, chopped

2 lb sweet potatoes, peeled and diced

4 cups vegetable broth

1 can coconut milk

2 tbsp extra virgin olive oil

1 tsp nutmeg

Directions:

Heat olive oil in a large saucepan over medium heat. Add onion and sauté until tender. Add in broth, sweet potato and nutmeg.

Bring to a boil then reduce heat and simmer, covered, for 30 minutes.

Blend soup until smooth and cook for 2-3 minutes until heated through.

Creamy Tomato and Roasted Pepper Soup

Serves: 4-5

Prep time: 35 min

Ingredients:

1 (12 oz) jar roasted red peppers, drained and chopped

1 onion, chopped

2 garlic cloves, minced

4 medium tomatoes, chopped

4 cups vegetable broth

3 tbsp extra virgin olive oil

2 bay leaves

Directions:

Heat olive oil in a large saucepan over medium-high heat and sauté onion for 3-4 minutes, stirring. Add in garlic and sauté until just fragrant. Stir in the red peppers, bay leaves and tomatoes and simmer for 10 minutes.

Add broth, season with salt and pepper and bring to the boil. Reduce heat and simmer for 20 minutes.

Set aside to cool slightly, remove the bay leaves and blend in batches, until smooth.

Fresh Asparagus Soup

Serves: 4-5

Prep time: 35 min

Ingredients:

2 lb fresh asparagus, cut into ½-inch pieces.

1 large onion, chopped

2 garlic cloves, minced

½ cup raw cashews, soaked in warm water for 1 hour

3 cups vegetable broth

3 tbsp extra virgin olive oil

lemon juice, to taste

Directions:

Heat olive oil in a large saucepan over medium-high heat and sauté onion for 3-4 minutes, stirring. Add in garlic and sauté until just fragrant. Stir in asparagus and simmer for 5 minutes. Add broth, season with salt and pepper and bring a the boil. Reduce heat and simmer for 20 minutes.

Set aside to cool slightly, add cashews, and blend, in batches, until smooth. Season with lemon juice and serve.

Shredded Cabbage Soup

Serves: 4-5

Prep time: 40 min

Ingredients:

1 onion, chopped

1/2 head cabbage, shredded

1 carrot, chopped

1 potato, peeled and diced

1 celery stalk, sliced

1 can (15 oz) diced tomatoes, undrained

3 cups vegetable broth

1 tsp Italian seasoning

3 tbsp extra virgin olive oil

salt and pepper, to taste

Directions:

Heat the oil over medium heat and gently sauté the onion until translucent. Add in cabbage, carrot, potato, celery, tomatoes, and seasoning and stir to combine.

Add in the broth, bring the soup to a boil, reduce heat, and simmer for 30-35 minutes. Season with salt and black pepper to taste.

Creamy Red Lentil Soup

Serves: 4-5

Prep time: 40 min

Ingredients:

1 cup red lentils

1/2 small onion, chopped

2 garlic cloves, chopped

1/2 red pepper, chopped

3 cups vegetable broth

1 cup coconut milk

3 tbsp extra virgin olive oil

1 tbsp paprika

1/2 tsp ginger

1 tsp cumin

salt and black pepper, to taste

Directions:

Gently heat olive oil in a large saucepan. Add onion, garlic, red pepper, paprika, ginger and cumin and sauté, stirring, until fragrant. Add in red lentils and vegetable broth.

Bring to a boil, cover, and simmer for 35 minutes. Add in coconut milk and simmer for 5 more minutes. Remove from heat, season with salt and black pepper, and blend until smooth. Serve hot.

Creamy Broccoli and Potato Soup

Serves: 4-5

Prep time: 30 min

Ingredients:

3 cups broccoli, chopped

2 potatoes, peeled and chopped

1 onion, chopped

3 garlic cloves, chopped

1 cup raw cashews

1 cup vegetable broth

4 cups water

3 tbsp extra virgin olive oil

1/2 tsp ground nutmeg

Directions:

Soak cashews in a bowl covered with water for at least 4 hours. Drain water and blend cashews with 1 cup of vegetable broth until smooth. Set aside.

Gently heat olive oil in a large saucepan over medium-high heat. Cook onion and garlic and for 3-4 minutes until tender. Add in broccoli, potato, nutmeg and water. Cover and bring to the boil, then reduce heat and simmer for 20 minutes, stirring from time to time.

Remove from heat and stir in cashew mixture. Blend until smooth, return to pan and cook until heated through.

Creamy Brussels Sprout Soup

Serves: 4-5

Prep time: 30 min

Ingredients:

1 lb frozen Brussels sprouts, thawed

2 potatoes, peeled and chopped

1 large onion, chopped

3 garlic cloves, minced

1 cup raw cashews

4 cups vegetable broth

3 tbsp extra virgin olive oil

1/2 tsp curry powder

salt and black pepper, to taste

Directions:

Soak cashews in a bowl covered with water for at least 4 hours. Drain water and blend cashews with 1 cup of vegetable broth until smooth. Set aside.

Gently heat olive oil in a large saucepan over medium-high heat. Cook onion and garlic and for 3-4 minutes until tender. Add in Brussels sprouts, potato, curry and vegetable broth. Cover and bring to a boil, then reduce heat and simmer for 20 minutes, stirring from time to time.

Remove from heat and stir in cashew mixture. Blend until smooth, return to pan and cook until heated through.

Creamy Potato Soup

Serves: 4-5

Prep time: 35 min

Ingredients:

6 medium potatoes, chopped

1 leek, white part only, chopped

1 carrot, chopped

1 zucchini, peeled and chopped

1 celery stalk, chopped

3 cups water

1 cup coconut milk

3 tbsp extra virgin olive oil

salt and black pepper, to taste

Directions:

Gently heat olive oil in a deep saucepan and sauté the onion for 2-3 minutes. Add in potatoes, carrot, zucchini and celery and cook for 2-3 minutes, stirring.

Add in water and salt, and bring to a boil then lower heat and simmer until the vegetables are tender.

Blend until smooth; add coconut milk, blend some more and serve.

Lentil, Barley and Kale Soup

Serves: 4-5

Prep time: 45 min

Ingredients:

2 medium leeks, chopped

3 garlic cloves, chopped

2 bay leaves

1 can tomatoes (15 oz), diced and undrained

1/2 cup red lentils

1/2 cup barley

1 bunch kale (10 oz), stemmed and coarsely chopped

4 cups water

3 tbsp extra virgin olive oil

1 tsp paprika

½ tsp cumin

Directions:

Heat oil in a large saucepan over medium-high heat. Sauté leeks and garlic until just fragrant. Add cumin and paprika, tomatoes, lentils, barley, and water. Season with salt and pepper.

Cover and bring to the boil then reduce heat and simmer for 40 minutes or until barley is tender.

Add in kale, stir it in, and simmer for five minutes more.

Mediterranean Lentil Soup

Serves: 4-5

Prep time: 40 min

Ingredients:

1/2 cup red lentils

2 carrots, chopped

1 onion, chopped

1 garlic clove, chopped

1 small red pepper, chopped

1 can tomatoes, chopped

½ can chickpeas, drained

½ can white beans, drained

1 celery stalk, chopped

6 cups water

1 tbsp paprika

1 tsp ginger, grated

1 tsp cumin

3 tbsp extra virgin olive oil

Directions:

Heat olive oil in a deep soup pot and gently sauté onions, garlic, red pepper and ginger. Add in water, lentils, chickpeas, white beans, tomatoes, carrots, celery, and cumin.

Bring to a boil then lower heat and simmer for 35 minutes, or until the lentils are tender. Purée half the soup in a food processor. Return the puréed soup to the pot, stir and serve.

Borscht

Serves: 4-5

Prep time: 90 min

Ingredients:

3 beets, peeled, quartered

1 carrot, peeled, chopped

1 large parsnip, peeled, cut into chunks

2 leeks, white part only, sliced

1/2 onion, chopped

1/4 cup lemon juice

1 tsp nutmeg

1 bay leaf

5 cups vegetable broth

1 cup vegan sour cream

1/2 cup fresh dill, finely cut

Directions:

Place all vegetables, spices, lemon juice and bay leaf in a large soup pot together with the vegetable broth. Bring to a boil, reduce the heat and simmer, partially covered, for 90 minutes.

Set aside to cool slightly and blend in batches. Season with salt and pepper, return to the pot and gently heat through. Serve in bowls, garnished with vegan sour cream and dill.

Celery, Apple and Carrot Soup

Serves: 4-5

Prep time: 20 min

Ingredients:

2 celery stalks, chopped

1 large apple, chopped

1/2 onion, chopped

2 carrots, chopped

1 garlic clove, minced

4 cups vegetable broth

3-4 tbsp extra virgin olive oil

1 tsp paprika

1 tsp grated ginger

salt and black pepper, to taste

Directions:

Heat olive oil in a deep soup pot over medium-high heat. Gently sauté onion, garlic and carrots for 3-4 minutes, stirring. Add in paprika, ginger, celery, apple and vegetable broth.

Bring to the boil then reduce heat and simmer, covered, for 15 minutes. Blend soup until smooth and return to pan. Cook over medium-high heat until heated through.

Season with salt and pepper to taste and serve.

Pea, Dill and Rice Soup

Serves: 4

Prep time: 20 min

Ingredients:

1 (16 oz) bag frozen green peas

1 onion, chopped

3-4 garlic cloves, chopped

1/3 cup rice

3 tbsp fresh dill, chopped

3 tbsp extra virgin olive oil

1/2 cup fresh dill, finely chopped, to serve

salt and pepper, to taste

Directions:

Heat oil in a large saucepan over medium-high heat and sauté onion and garlic for 3-4 minutes.

Add in peas and vegetable broth and bring to the boil. Stir in rice, cover, reduce heat, and simmer for 20 minutes.

Add dill, season with salt and pepper and serve sprinkled with fresh dill.

Minted Pea and Nettle Soup

Serves: 4

Prep time: 20 min

Ingredients:

1 onion, chopped

3-4 garlic cloves, chopped

4 cups vegetable broth

2 tbsp dried mint leaves

1 16 oz bag frozen green peas

about 20 nettle tops

3 tbsp extra virgin olive oil

1 cup fresh dill, finely chopped, to serve

Directions:

Heat oil in a large saucepan over medium-high heat and sauté onion and garlic for 3-4 minutes.

Add in dried mint, peas, washed nettles, and vegetable broth and bring to the boil. Cover, reduce heat, and simmer for 15 minutes.

Remove from heat and set aside to cool slightly, then blend in batches, until smooth. Return soup to saucepan over medium-low heat and cook until heated through.

Season with salt and pepper. Serve sprinkled with fresh dill.

Bean and Spinach Soup

Serves: 4-5

Prep time: 20 min

Ingredients:

1 onion, chopped

1 large carrot, chopped

2 garlic cloves, minced

1 15 oz can white beans, rinsed and drained

1 cup spinach leaves, trimmed and washed

3 cups vegetable broth

1 tbsp paprika

1 tbsp dried mint

3 tbsp extra virgin olive oil

salt and black pepper, to taste

Directions:

Heat the olive oil over medium heat and gently sauté the onion, garlic and carrot. Add in beans, broth, salt and pepper and bring to a boil.

Reduce heat and cook for 15 minutes, or until the carrots are tender. Stir in spinach, and simmer for about 5 minutes, until spinach wilts.

Italian Minestrone

Serves: 4-5

Prep time: 25 min

Ingredients:

1/2 onion, chopped

2 garlic cloves, chopped

¼ cabbage, chopped

1 carrot, chopped

2 celery stalks, chopped

3 cups water

1 cup canned tomatoes, diced, undrained

1 1/2 cup green beans, trimmed and cut into 1/2-inch pieces

1/2 cup pasta, cooked

2-3 fresh basil leaves

2 tbsp extra virgin olive oil

black pepper and salt, to taste

Directions:

Heat the olive oil in a large pot over medium-high heat. Add the onion and cook until translucent, about 4 minutes. Add in garlic, carrot and celery and cook for 5 minutes more.

Stir in the green beans, cabbage, tomatoes, basil, and water and bring to a boil.

Reduce heat and simmer uncovered, for 15 minutes, or until the vegetables are tender. Stir in pasta, season with pepper and salt to taste and serve.

French Vegetable Soup

Serves: 4-5

Prep time: 30 min

Ingredients:

2 leeks, white and pale green parts only, well rinsed and thinly sliced

1 large zucchini, peeled and diced

1 medium fennel bulb, trimmed, cored, and cut into large chunks

2 garlic cloves, chopped

3 cups vegetable broth

1 cup canned tomatoes, drained and chopped

1/2 cup vermicelli, broken into small pieces

3 tbsp extra virgin olive oil

black pepper, to taste

Directions:

Heat the olive oil in a large soup pot. Add the leeks and cook over low heat for 5 minutes. Add in the zucchini, fennel and garlic and cook for about 5 minutes. Stir in the vegetable broth and the tomatoes and bring to the boil.

Reduce heat and simmer, uncovered, for 20 minutes, or until the vegetables are tender but still holding their shape. Stir in the vermicelli. Simmer for a further 5 minutes and serve.

Spiced Beet and Carrot Soup

Serves: 4-5

Prep time: 25 min

Ingredients:

3 beets, washed and peeled

2 carrots, peeled and chopped

1 small onion, chopped

1 garlic clove, chopped

3 cups vegetable broth

1 cup water

2 tbsp extra virgin olive oil

1 tsp grated ginger

1 tsp grated orange peel

Directions:

Heat the olive oil in a large soup pot. Add the onion and sauté over low heat for 3-4 minutes or until translucent. Add the garlic, beets, carrots, ginger and lemon rind. Stir in water and vegetable broth and bring to the boil.

Reduce heat to medium and simmer, partially covered, for 30 minutes, or until the beets are tender. Cool slightly and blend soup in batches until smooth. Season with salt and pepper and serve.

Cauliflower Soup

Serves: 4-5

Prep time: 35 min

Ingredients:

1 medium head cauliflower, chopped

1 garlic clove, minced

3 cups vegetable broth

1 cup coconut milk

3-4 tbsp extra virgin olive oil

salt, to taste

black pepper, to taste

Directions:

Heat the olive oil in a deep soup pot over medium heat and gently sauté the cauliflower for 4-5 minutes. Stir in the garlic and vegetable broth and bring to a boil.

Reduce heat, cover, and simmer for 30 minutes. Add in coconut milk and blend in a blender until smooth. Season with salt and pepper to taste and serve.

Pumpkin and Bell Pepper Soup

Serves: 4-5

Prep time: 35 min

Ingredients:

1/2 small onion, chopped

3 cups diced pumpkin

2 red bell peppers, chopped

1 carrot, chopped

3 cups vegetable broth

3 tbsp extra virgin olive oil

1/2 tsp cumin

salt and black pepper, to taste

Directions:

Heat the olive oil in a deep soup pot and sauté the onion for 4-5 minutes. Add in the pumpkin, carrot, and bell peppers, and cook, stirring, for 5 minutes. Stir in broth and cumin and bring to the boil.

Reduce heat to low, cover, and simmer, stirring occasionally, for 30 minutes, or until vegetables are soft. Season with salt and pepper, blend in batches and reheat to serve.

Wild Mushroom Soup

Serves: 4-5

Prep time: 35 min

Ingredients:

2 lbs mixed wild mushrooms, chopped

1 large onion, chopped

2 garlic cloves, minced

3 cups vegetable broth

1 tsp dried thyme

salt and pepper, to taste

3 tbsp extra virgin olive oil

Directions:

Sauté onions and garlic in a large soup pot until transparent. Add thyme and mushrooms.

Stir, and cook for 10 minutes, then add the vegetable broth and simmer for another 10-20 minutes. Blend, season and serve.

Mushroom and Kale Soup

Serves: 4-5

Prep time: 30 min

Ingredients:

1 onion, chopped

1 carrot, chopped

1 zucchini, peeled and diced

1 potato, peeled and diced

10 white mushrooms, chopped

1 bunch kale (10 oz), stemmed and coarsely chopped

3 cups vegetable broth

4 tbsp extra virgin olive oil

salt and black pepper. to taste

Directions:

Gently heat olive oil in a large soup pot. Add in onions, carrot and mushrooms and cook until vegetables are tender. Stir in zucchini, kale and vegetable broth.

Season to taste with salt and pepper, and simmer for 20 minutes.

Spinach and Pasta Soup

Serves: 4-5

Prep time: 35 min

Ingredients:

14 oz frozen spinach, slightly thawed

1 small onion, chopped

1 small carrot, chopped

1 large tomato, diced

1/2 cup dry pasta

5 cups hot water

4 tbsp extra virgin olive oil

1 tbsp paprika

salt and black pepper, to taste

salt, to taste

Directions:

Heat oil in a deep cooking pot. Add in the onion and carrot and cook for 3-4 minutes, until tender. Add in paprika, spinach, tomato, and water and stir. Season with salt and black pepper and bring to a boil.

Add in pasta, reduce heat, and simmer for around 30 minutes.

Lemon Artichoke Soup

Serves: 4-5

Prep time: 35 min

Ingredients:

3 cups artichoke hearts, chopped

1/2 onion, chopped

1 celery stalk, chopped

1 carrot, chopped

2 garlic cloves, minced

2 cups vegetable broth

2 tbsp olive oil

1 tsp salt

2 tbsp lemon juice

1 cup coconut milk

Directions:

Heat olive oil in a large pot and gently sauté the onion, celery, carrot, and garlic until the onion and garlic are translucent. Stir in vegetable broth, artichokes and salt and bring to the boil.

Reduce heat, add lemon juice and simmer for 15 minutes. Set aside to cool and blend until smooth. Stir in coconut milk and simmer for another 5 minutes.

Quinoa, Sweet Potato and Tomato Soup

Serves: 4

Prep time: 25 min

Ingredients:

½ cup quinoa

1 onion, chopped

1 large sweet potato, peeled and chopped

½ cup canned chickpeas, drained

1 cup baby spinach leaves

1 can tomatoes, drained and diced

3 cups vegetable broth

1 cup water

2 cloves garlic, chopped

1 tbsp grated fresh ginger

1 tsp cumin

1 tbsp paprika

2 tbsp extra virgin olive oil

Directions:

Wash quinoa very well, drain and set aside.

In a large soup pot, heat the olive oil over medium heat. Add the onions and garlic and sauté about 1-2 minutes, stirring. Add the sweet potato and sauté for another minute then add in the paprika, ginger and cumin.

Add water and broth, bring to a boil and stir in quinoa and

Red Lentil and Quinoa Soup

Serves: 4

Prep time: 35 min

Ingredients:

½ cup quinoa

1 cup red lentils

5 cups water

1 onion, chopped

2-3 garlic cloves, chopped

½ red bell pepper, finely cut

1 small tomato, chopped

3 tbsp extra virgin olive oil

1 tsp ginger

1 tsp cumin

1 tbsp paprika

salt and black pepper, to taste

Directions:

Wash and drain quinoa and red lentils and set aside.

In a large soup pot, heat the olive oil over medium heat. Add in the onion, garlic and red pepper and sauté for 1-2 minutes, stirring. Add the paprika and spices and stir. Add in the red lentils and quinoa, stir and add the water.

Gently bring to the boil, then lower heat and simmer, covered for 25 minutes. Add the tomato and cook for five more minutes. Blend the soup, serve and enjoy!

Spinach and Quinoa Soup

Serves: 4-5

Prep time: 20 min

Ingredients:

½ cup quinoa

1 onion, chopped

1 garlic clove, chopped

1 small zucchini, peeled and diced

1 tomato, diced

2 cups fresh spinach, cut

4 cups water

3 tbsp extra virgin olive oil

1 tbsp paprika

salt and pepper, to taste

Directions:

Heat olive oil in a deep soup pot over medium-high heat. Add onion and garlic and sauté for 1 minute, stirring constantly. Add in paprika and zucchini, stir, and cook for 2-3 minutes more.

Add 4 cups of water and bring to a boil then add in spinach and quinoa. Stir and reduce heat. Simmer for 15 minutes then set aside to cool.

Vegetable Quinoa Soup

Serves: 4-5

Prep time: 25 min

Ingredients:

½ cup quinoa

1 cup sliced leeks

1 garlic clove, chopped

½ carrot, diced

1 tomato, diced

1 small zucchini, diced

½ cup frozen green beans

4 cups water

1 tsp paprika

4 tbsp extra virgin olive oil

5-6 tbsp lemon juice, to serve

Directions:

Wash quinoa in a fine sieve under running water until the water runs clear. Set aside to drain.

Heat olive oil in a soup pot and gently sauté the leeks, garlic and carrot for 1 minute, stirring. Add in paprika, zucchini, tomatoes, green beans and water.

Bring to a boil, add quinoa and lower heat to medium-low. Simmer for 20 minutes, or until the vegetables are tender. Serve with lemon juice.

Tomato and Quinoa Soup

Serves: 4-5

Prep time: 35 min

Ingredients:

4 cups chopped fresh tomatoes

1 onion, chopped

1/3 cup quinoa

2 cups water

1 garlic clove, minced

3 tbsp extra virgin olive oil

1 tbsp paprika

1 tsp salt

½ tsp black pepper

1 tbsp sugar

fresh parsley, chopped, to serve

Directions:

Heat olive oil in a large soup pot and sauté onions until translucent. Add in paprika, garlic and tomatoes and water and bring to the boil.

Simmer for 10 minutes, blend the soup and return it to the pot. Add the very well washed quinoa and a tablespoon of sugar and bring to the boil again.

Simmer for 15 minutes stirring occasionally. Serve sprinkled with parsley.

Kale, Leek and Quinoa Soup

Serves: 4-5

Prep time: 35 min

Ingredients:

½ cup quinoa

2 leeks, white part only, chopped

1/2 onion, chopped

1 can tomatoes, diced and undrained

1 bunch kale (10 oz), stemmed and coarsely chopped

4 cups vegetable broth

3 tbsp extra virgin olive oil

salt and pepper, to taste

Directions:

Heat olive oil in a large pot over medium heat and gently sauté the onion for 3-4 minutes. Add in the leeks, season with salt and pepper, and add the vegetable broth, tomatoes and quinoa.

Bring to a boil then reduce heat and simmer for 15 minutes. Stir in kale and cook for another 5 minutes.

Potato, Pea and Cauliflower Curry

Serves: 4

Prep time: 25 min

Ingredients:

1 lb potatoes, peeled and cubed

1 lb cauliflower, cut into small florets

1 cup fresh peas

1 onion, finely chopped

2 garlic cloves, crushed

1 cup vegetable broth

1 tsp finely grated fresh ginger

1 tbsp curry powder

2 tbsp extra virgin olive oil

1/2 cup tomato pasta sauce

1/2 cup coconut milk

1 tsp cornflour

Directions:

Heat oil in a large saucepan over medium heat. Add the onion and gently sauté, stirring, for 3-4 minutes until transparent. Add in garlic and ginger, and cook for 1 minute until just fragrant. Add in the curry powder, potatoes and cauliflower florets, and stir.

Add in broth and tomato sauce and simmer, uncovered, for 15-20 minutes or until the potatoes are tender.

Combine the coconut milk and cornflour in a small bowl. Gradually add to the potato mixture, stirring constantly. Add the peas, reduce heat, and simmer for 2 minutes or until the peas are tender and the mixture is heated through. Serve with rice.

Cauliflower with Chilli and Mustard

Serves: 4

Prep time: 25 min

Ingredients:

2 lbs cauliflower, cut into small florets

3 long fresh green chillies, thinly sliced

1 onion, finely chopped

2 garlic cloves, crushed

1/2 cup vegetable broth

2 teaspoons mustard seeds

1 tsp ground turmeric

1 tsp tamarind paste

2 tbsp extra virgin olive oil

Directions:

Heat oil in a large saucepan over medium heat. Add the onion and gently sauté, stirring, for 3-4 minutes until transparent. Add in garlic and chilli, and cook for 1 minute until just fragrant. Add the mustard seeds and turmeric and sauté, stirring, for 20 seconds or until the mustard seeds pop.

Add the cauliflower and stir to coat. Add the vegetable broth and tamarind paste and simmer for 4 minutes or until the cauliflower is tender crisp. Season with salt to taste ans serve.

Baked Cauliflower

Serves: 4

Prep time: 25 min

Ingredients:

1 small cauliflower, cut into florets

1 tbsp garlic powder

1 tsp paprika

salt, to taste

black pepper, to taste

4 tbsp extra virgin olive oil

Directions:

Combine olive oil, paprika, salt, pepper and garlic powder together. Toss in the cauliflower florets and place in a baking dish in one layer. Bake in a preheated to 350 F oven for 20 minutes or until golden.

Maple Roast Parsnip with Pear and Sage

Serves: 4

Prep time: 65 min

Ingredients:

5 parsnips, peeled, halved, cut into large wedges

2 large pears, cut into wedges

1 large onion, cut into wedges

1 tbsp garlic powder

1/3 cup fresh sage leaves

2 tablespoons maple syrup

1/4 teaspoon dried chilli flakes

4 tbsp extra virgin olive oil

Directions:

Preheat oven to 350F. Line 2 baking trays with baking paper. Place the parsnip, pear, onion, and sage on the prepared trays.

Combine the maple syrup, olive oil, garlic powder and dried chilli flakes in a bowl.

Pour the maple mixture evenly over the parsnip mixture and gently toss to combine. Bake, turning halfway during cooking, for 1 hour or until the parsnip is golden and tender.

Balsamic Roasted Carrots and Baby Onions

Serves: 4

Prep time: 50 min

Ingredients:

2 bunches baby carrots, scrubbed, ends trimmed

10 small onions, peeled, halved

4 tbsp brown sugar

1 tsp thyme

3 tbsp balsamic vinegar

2 tbsp extra virgin olive oil

Directions:

Preheat oven to 350F. Line a baking tray with baking paper.

Place the carrots, onion, thyme and oil in a large bowl and toss until well coated. Arrange carrots and onion, in a single layer, on the baking tray. Roast for 25 minutes or until tender.

Sprinkle over the sugar and vinegar and toss to coat. Roast for 25-30 minutes more or until vegetables are tender and caramelized. Season with salt and pepper to taste and serve.

Potato and Zucchini Bake

Serves: 5-6

Prep time: 25 min

Ingredients:

1 lb potatoes, peeled and sliced

4-5 zucchinis, peeled and sliced

1 onion, sliced

2 garlic cloves, crushed

½ cup water

4 tbsp extra virgin olive oil

1 tsp dry oregano

1/3 cup fresh dill, chopped

salt and black pepper, to taste

Directions:

Place the potatoes, zucchinis and onion in a shallow ovenproof baking dish. Pour over the olive oil and water. Add salt, black pepper to taste, and toss everything together.

Bake in a preheated to 350 F oven for 40 minutes, stirring halfway through, bake for 5 minutes more and serve.

One-Pot Vegan Pizza

Serves: 4

Prep time: 50 min

Ingredients:

1 store-bought or homemade dough

3-4 green onions, chopped

1 cup white button mushrooms, chopped

1/2 cup red bell pepper, chopped

1 garlic clove, chopped

1 cup sweet corn

1/2 cup fresh tomato sauce

1/2 cup vegan cheese

3 tbsp olive oil

1 tbsp dried basil

salt and black pepper, to taste

Directions:

Heat a large skillet on medium heat and sauté the onion and bell pepper for 2-3 minutes until fragrant. Add in the mushrooms, garlic, corn and basil and sauté for 5 minutes more. Season with salt and black pepper to taste.

Roll out dough onto a floured surface and transfer to a parchment-lined 12 inch round baking sheet (or pizza stone).

Top it with tomato sauce, vegan cheese and the sautéed vegetables.

Bake for 30 minutes in a preheated to 450 F oven or until the crust is golden brown and the sauce is bubbly. Set aside for 5 minutes, cut, and serve.

One-Pot Vegan Pasta

Serves: 4-5

Ingredients:

12 oz dry pasta

1/2 onion, chopped

1/2 small eggplant, peeled and cubed

1 small zucchini, peeled and cubed

1 garlic clove, crushed

1.5 cups vegan marinara sauce

2 cups water

3 tbsp olive oil

1/3 cup fresh parsley, finely cut

1 tsp salt

1 tsp fresh black pepper

Directions:

Heat a large saucepan over medium-high heat. Add in olive oil and gently sauté the onion. Stir in eggplant, garlic, the zucchini, pasta, water, marinara sauce, and season with salt and black pepper. Bring to a boil, then cover and reduce heat to a simmer until the pasta is cooked to al dente. Sprinkle with parsley, adjust seasonings, and serve.

Easy One-Pot Spaghetti

Serves: 4-5

Prep time: 35 min

Ingredients:

12 oz spaghetti

1/2 onion, chopped

1 small zucchini, peeled and chopped

1/2 can chickpeas, drained

1/2 cup sweet corn

2 garlic cloves, crushed

1.5 cups vegan marinara sauce

2 cups water

3 tbsp olive oil

1/3 cup fresh parsley, finely cut

1 tsp salt

Directions:

Heat a large saucepan over medium-high heat. Add in olive oil and gently sauté the onion. Stir in garlic, chickpeas, sweet corn, zucchini, water, marinara sauce, and season with salt and black pepper.

Bring to a boil, then add spaghetti and stir. Reduce heat and simmer until the spaghetti is cooked to al dente. Sprinkle with parsley, adjust seasonings, and serve.

Lentil and Olive Spaghetti

Serves: 4-5

Prep time: 35 min

Ingredients:

12 oz spaghetti

1/2 onion, chopped

1 can brown lentils, rinsed, drained

1 cup black olives, pitted and halved

2 garlic cloves, crushed

2 cups vegan marinara sauce

2 cups water

3 tbsp olive oil

1/3 cup fresh mint, finely cut

1 tsp salt

Directions:

Heat a large saucepan over medium-high heat. Add in olive oil and gently sauté the onion. Stir in garlic, lentils, olives, water, marinara sauce, and season with salt and black pepper.

Bring to a boil, then add spaghetti and stir. Reduce heat and simmer until the spaghetti is cooked to al dente. Sprinkle with mint, adjust seasonings, and serve.

Summer Zucchini Risotto

Serves 4

Prep time: 25 min

Ingredients:

3 small zucchinis, peeled and diced

4-5 spring onions, finely chopped

2 medium tomatoes, diced

1 cup risotto rice

1/2 cup frozen peas

2 ½ cups vegetable broth

2 tbsp extra virgin olive oil

1 tsp salt

1 tsp paprika

1 bunch fresh dill

Directions:

In a deep saucepan, heat olive oil and gently sauté green onions, stirring. Add in zucchinis, tomatoes, peas, rice, salt, paprika, and half the vegetable broth.

Stir and cook for 10 min or until the liquid has evaporated, stirring from time to time. Add the rest of the broth, then continue to cook for a further 5 min. Sprinkle with dill and serve.

Vegetable Quinoa Stew

Serves: 4-5

Prep time: 20 min

Ingredients:

1 cup quinoa

1 ½ cup water

1 onion, finely cut

2 red bell peppers, chopped

1 zucchini, peeled and chopped

1 cup fresh green peas

1 tomato, chopped

2 garlic cloves, chopped

1 tbsp paprika

3 tbsp extra virgin olive oil

½ cup fresh dill, finely cut, to serve

Directions:

Rinse the quinoa very well in a sieve under running water and set aside to drain.

Heat olive oil in large saucepan over medium-high heat. Add the onion and sauté for 1-2 minutes. Add in the garlic, paprika, bell pepper, green peas and zucchini.

Cook, stirring occasionally, for 5 minutes then add the tomato and the water. Bring to the boil and add in quinoa. Stir, cover, and cook for 15 minutes. Season with salt to taste and serve sprinkled with dill.

Eggplant and Quinoa Stew

Serves: 4-5

Prep time: 20 min

Ingredients:

1 cup quinoa

1 ½ cups water

1 large eggplant, peeled and diced

1 cup canned tomatoes, drained and diced

1 zucchini, diced

5-6 black olives, pitted and halved

1 onion, chopped

4 garlic cloves, chopped

1 tbsp tomato paste

3 tbsp extra virgin olive oil

1 tsp paprika

salt and black pepper, to taste

½ cup parsley leaves, finely cut, to serve

Directions:

Rinse the quinoa very well in a fine sieve under running water and set aside to drain.

Gently sauté onions, garlic and eggplant in olive oil on medium-high heat for 5-6 minutes. Add in paprika and tomato paste and stir for 1-2 minutes.

Add in the rest of the vegetables and the water; and bring to the boil.

Stir in quinoa, lower heat and simmer, covered, for 15 minutes. Sprinkle with parsley and serve.

Comforting Quinoa Shepherd's Stew

Serves: 4-5

Prep time: 20 min

Ingredients:

1 cup quinoa

1 ½ cups water

1 onion, finely cut

2 garlic cloves, chopped

2 red peppers, chopped

2 carrots, chopped

1 large potato, diced

6-7 white mushrooms, chopped

1-2 tomatoes, diced

2 tbsp extra virgin olive oil

1 tbsp paprika

1 bay leaf

1 tbsp thyme

1 tsp summer savory

Directions:

Wash quinoa very well, drain and set aside.

In a large soup pot or casserole dish, heat the oil over medium heat. Add the onion, bell peppers and garlic and sauté until softened, about 3 minutes. Stir in the paprika. bay leaf, thyme and savory and stir.

Add the other vegetables and mushrooms and cook for 1-2 minutes, stirring. Add in water and bring to the boil then stir in the quinoa.

Reduce heat to low and simmer, covered, for 15-20 minutes.

Easy Moroccan Vegetable Stew with Quinoa

Serves: 6

Prep time: 20 min

Ingredients:

1 large onion, chopped

2 garlic cloves, chopped

1 cup quinoa

2 cups vegetable broth

1 cup canned chickpeas, drained

1 cup canned tomatoes, diced and undrained

1 carrot, chopped

1 cup baby spinach leaves

¼ cup dried prunes

¼ cup dried apricots

1 zucchini, quartered lengthwise and chopped

½ cup almonds, coarsely chopped

3 tbsp extra virgin olive oil

1 tsp grated ginger

1 tsp ground cinnamon

Directions:

In a large soup pot or casserole dish, heat the oil over medium heat. Add the onion, ginger, garlic and cinnamon and sauté for 2-3 minutes, or until the onion has softened.

Add in the vegetable broth, chickpeas, tomatoes, carrots, apricots and prunes and bring to a boil. Stir in add quinoa and zucchinis, reduce heat and simmer, covered, for 15 minutes.

Add in the baby spinach and cook until it wilts. Add the almonds, stir and serve.

Zucchini and Buckwheat Stew

Serves: 4-5

Prep time: 20 min

Ingredients:

1 cup toasted buckwheat groats

1 ½ cups vegetable broth

1 onion, finely chopped

3 garlic cloves, chopped

4 zucchinis, peeled and diced

1 cup fresh dill, finely cut

3 tbsp extra virgin olive oil

salt, to taste

Directions:

In a deep saucepan, heat olive oil and gently sauté the onion and garlic for 1-2 minutes. Add the diced zucchinis and sauté for 5-6 minutes, stirring.

Add in vegetable broth and bring to the boil. Stir in the toasted buckwheat, finely cut dill and salt to taste, and simmer for 15-20 minutes.

Power Buckwheat Stew

Serves: 4-5

Prep time: 20 min

Ingredients:

1 cup toasted buckwheat groats

1 cup vegetable broth or water

1 onion, chopped

1 potato, chopped

1 zucchini, peeled and chopped

1 tomato, diced

½ cup frozen corn kernels

½ cup frozen peas

½ cup black olives, halved, pitted

2 garlic cloves, minced

4 tbsp extra virgin olive oil

salt and pepper, to taste

1 cup parsley, finely cut

Directions:

In a deep saucepan, heat olive oil and gently sauté the onion and garlic for a minute. Add in the green peas, potato, zucchini, corn, olives and cook, stirring for 3-4 minutes.

Add water or vegetable broth and bring to the boil. Stir in the diced tomato and the toasted buckwheat. Reduce heat, cover, and simmer for 10 minutes, stirring occasionally. Serve sprinkled with parsley and enjoy!

Quick Buckwheat Chilli

Serves: 4-5

Prep time: 20-25 min

Ingredients:

1 cup toasted buckwheat groats

1 ¾ cups vegetable broth

1 large onion, finely cut

3 cloves garlic, chopped

1 green bell pepper, chopped

1 can diced tomatoes

1 can mixed beans, well rinsed and drained

1 tbsp paprika

1 tsp chilli powder

1 tsp ground cumin

2 tbsp extra virgin olive oil

¼ cup chopped fresh coriander, to serve

Directions:

In a large soup pot or casserole dish, heat the oil over medium heat. Add the onion, bell pepper and garlic and sauté until softened, about 3 minutes. Stir in the chilli powder, cumin and paprika and sauté for another minute.

Add the buckwheat and stir to combine well. Stir in the tomatoes, beans and vegetable broth. Bring to a boil then reduce heat to low and simmer, covered, for about 20 minutes.

Serve sprinkled with fresh coriander.

Ratatouille

Serves: 4

Prep time: 45 min

Ingredients:

1 eggplant, peeled and diced

2 large tomatoes, diced

2 zucchinis, peeled and sliced

1 onion, sliced

1 green pepper, sliced

6-7 mushrooms, sliced

3 cloves garlic, crushed

1 tbsp dried parsley

3 tbsp extra virgin olive oil

salt, to taste

Directions:

Place eggplant on a tray and sprinkle it with salt. Set aside for 30 minutes, then rinse and pat dry.

Heat olive oil in an ovenproof casserole dish over medium heat. Gently sauté the garlic until fragrant. Add in parsley and eggplant and cook until the eggplant is soft.

Spread zucchinis in an even layer over the eggplant. Layer onion, mushrooms, pepper and tomatoes, and bake in a preheated to 350 F oven for 40 minutes.

Okra and Tomato Casserole

Serves: 4

Prep time: 25 min

Ingredients:

1 lb okra, trimmed

3 tomatoes, cut into wedges

3 garlic cloves, chopped

1 cup fresh parsley leaves, finely cut

3 tbsp extra virgin olive oil

1 tsp salt

black pepper, to taste

Directions:

In a deep ovenproof baking dish, combine okra, sliced tomatoes, olive oil and garlic. Add in salt and black pepper to taste, and toss to combine.

Bake in a preheated to 350 F oven for 45 minutes, or until the okra is tender. Sprinkle with parsley and serve.

Spicy Chickpea and Spinach Stew

Serves: 4

Prep time: 40 min

Ingredients:

1 onion, chopped

3 garlic cloves, chopped

1 15 oz can chickpeas, drained and rinsed

1 15 oz can tomatoes, diced and undrained

1 1 lb bag baby spinach

a handful of blanched almonds

½ cup vegetable broth

1 tbsp hot chilli paste

½ tsp cumin

salt and pepper, to taste

Directions:

Heat olive oil in a large saucepan over medium-high heat. Gently sauté onion and garlic for 4-5 minutes, or until tender. Add spices and stir. Add in chickpeas, tomatoes, almonds and broth.

Bring to a boil, then reduce heat to low and simmer, partially covered, for 10 minutes. Add the chilli paste and spinach to the pot and stir until the spinach wilts. Remove from heat and season with salt and pepper to taste.

Moroccan Chickpea Stew

Serves: 4-5

Prep time: 20 min

Ingredients:

1 onion, chopped

3 garlic cloves, chopped

2 large carrots, chopped

2 sweet potatoes, peeled and chopped

4-5 dates, pitted and chopped

1 cup spinach, chopped

1 15 oz can tomatoes, diced and undrained

1 15 oz can chickpeas, rinsed and drained

1 cup vegetable broth

1 tbsp ground cumin

½ tsp chilli powder

½ tsp ground turmeric

½ teaspoon salt

3 tbsp extra virgin olive oil

½ cup chopped cilantro, to serve

grated lemon zest, to serve

Directions:

Heat olive oil in a large saucepan over medium-high heat. Gently sauté onion, garlic and carrots for 4-5 minutes, or until tender. Add all spices and stir. Stir in all other ingredients except the spinach.

Bring to a boil, cover, reduce heat, and simmer for 20 minutes, or until potatoes are tender. Add in spinach, stir and cook it until it wilts.

Serve over brown rice, quinoa or couscous and top with chopped cilantro and lemon zest.

Chickpea, Rice and Mushroom Stew

Serves: 4-5

Prep time: 20-30 min

Ingredients:

1 15 oz can chickpeas, drained

1 large onion, finely cut

2 cups mushrooms, chopped

2 carrots, chopped

1 15 oz can tomatoes, diced, undrained

1/3 cup rice, washed

1 cup vegetable broth

4 tbsp extra virgin olive oil

1 tsp oregano

1 tbsp paprika

1 cup fresh parsley, finely cut

1 tbsp sugar

Directions:

In a deep, heavy-bottomed saucepan, heat olive oil and gently sauté the onion and carrots for 4-5 minutes, stirring constantly. Add in paprika, chickpeas, rice, mushrooms, tomatoes, sugar and vegetable broth and stir again.

Season with salt, oregano, ground black pepper and bring to the boil. Cover, reduce heat, and simmer for about 20 minutes, stirring from time to time. Sprinkle with parsley, simmer for a minute more and serve.

Easy Chickpea Dinner

Serves: 4-5

Prep time: 20 min

Ingredients:

1 large onion, chopped

15-20 black olives, pitted

2 zucchinis, peeled and diced

1 15 oz can chickpeas, drained

1 cup marinara sauce

1/2 cup fresh parsley leaves, finely cut

4 tbsp extra virgin olive oil

salt and black pepper, to taste

Directions:

In a deep saucepan, heat olive oil and sauté the onion for 2-3 minutes. Add in the chickpeas, zucchinis, olives and marinara sauce.

Season with black pepper, and simmer on medium-high for 30 minutes. Sprinkle with parsley and serve.

Baked Bean and Rice Casserole

Serves: 4-5

Prep time: 30 min

Ingredients:

2 cans (15 oz) white or red beans, drained

1 cup water or vegetable broth

2/3 cup rice

2 onions, chopped

1 cup parsley, finely cut

7-8 fresh mint leaves, finely cut

3 tbsp extra virgin olive oil

1 tbsp paprika

½ tsp black pepper

1 tsp salt

Directions:

Heat olive oil in an ovenproof casserole dish and gently sauté the chopped onions for 1-2 minutes. Stir in paprika and rice and cook, stirring constantly, for another minute.

Add in beans and a cup of water or vegetable broth, season with salt and black pepper, stir in mint and parsley, and bake in a preheated to 350 F oven for 20 minutes.

Green Pea and Rice Casserole

Serves: 4-5

Prep time: 20 min

Ingredients:

1 onion, chopped

1 1 lb bag frozen peas

3 garlic cloves, chopped

3-4 mushrooms, chopped

2/3 cup white rice

1 cup water

4 tbsp extra virgin olive oil

salt and black pepper, to taste

Directions:

In a deep ovenproof casserole dish, heat olive oil and sauté the onions, garlic and mushrooms for 2-3 minutes. Add in the rice and cook, stirring constantly for 1 minute.

Add in a cup of warm water and the frozen peas, stir, bake in a preheated to 350 F oven for 20 minutes, and serve.

Easy Green Bean Stew

Serves: 4-5

Prep time: 20 min

Ingredients:

2 10 oz bags frozen green beans

1 large onion, finely cut

2 carrots, sliced

1 tomato, diced

3-4 garlic cloves, chopped

1 cup fresh dill, finely chopped

1 tbsp chia seeds

4 tbsp extra virgin olive oil

1 tsp salt

1 tbsp paprika

Directions:

Heat olive oil in a deep casserole dish and gently sauté the onions and the garlic. Add in the paprika and carrots and stir. Add the green beans and the tomato.

Bring to the boil then lower heat and simmer, covered, for about 30 minutes. Sprinkle with chia seeds, fresh dill, and serve.

Green Beans and Potatoes

Serves: 4-5

Prep time: 20 min

Ingredients:

1 bag frozen green beans

3 potatoes, peeled and diced

1 tsp tomato paste

1 carrot, sliced

1 onion, chopped

2 garlic cloves, crushed

3 tbsp extra virgin olive oil

1/2 cup fresh dill, finely chopped

½ cup water

1 tsp paprika

salt and pepper, to taste

Directions:

Heat olive oil in a deep saucepan and sauté the onion for 2-3 minutes, stirring. Add in garlic and sauté until just fragrant. Add in the green beans, and all remaining ingredients.

Stir to combine very well, cover, and simmer for about 20-30 minutes until all vegetables are tender. Serve warm sprinkled with fresh dill.

Cabbage and Rice Stew

Serves: 4

Prep time: 25 min

Ingredients:

1 cup white rice

½ medium head cabbage, cored and shredded

1 small onion, chopped

2 tomatoes, diced

1 cup hot water

2 tbsp extra virgin olive oil

1 tbsp paprika

1 tsp cumin

salt, to taste

black pepper, to taste

Directions:

Heat olive oil in a large ovenproof baking dish and gently sauté onion until transparent. Add in paprika, cumin, rice and water, stir, and bring to a boil.

Simmer for 5 minutes then add in the shredded cabbage and tomatoes.

Stir to combine well and bake in a preheated to 350 F oven for about 20 minutes, stirring occasionally.

Season with salt and black pepper to taste, and set aside for 4-5 minutes. Serve sprinkled with fresh parsley.

Hearty Slow Cooker Baked Beans

Serves: 8-10

Prep time: 4 hours

Ingredients:

12 oz dried white beans

1 large onion, finely cut

1 red bell pepper, chopped

1 carrot, chopped

1 tomato, diced

water for soaking the beans

1 1/2 cups water

1 tbsp paprika

1/2 tsp black pepper

1 cup parsley, finely cut

1 cup mint, finely cut

1 tsp salt

Directions:

Wash the beans and soak them in water overnight. In the morning discard the water.

Combine all ingredients in slow cooker. Cover and cook on high setting for 4 hours, stirring occasionally.

Slow Cooker Stuffed Bell Peppers

Serves: 4-5

Prep time: 5-6 hours

Ingredients:

8 bell peppers, cored and seeded

1 1/2 cups rice

1 large onion, finely cut

1 ripe tomato, diced

1/2 cup fresh parsley, chopped

2 cups warm water

3 tbsp extra virgin olive oil

1 tbsp paprika

salt and pepper, to taste

Directions:

Heat the olive oil and sauté the onion for 2-3 minutes. Add in paprika, rice and the diced tomato and season with salt and pepper. Add ½ cup of hot water and cook the rice, stirring, until the water is absorbed.

Stuff each pepper with rice mixture using a spoon. Every pepper should be ¾ full. Arrange the peppers in a slow cooker and top up with the remaining warm water.

Cover and cook for 5-6 hours on low setting.

FREE BONUS RECIPES: 25 Superfood Paleo and Vegan Smoothies for Vibrant Health and Easy Weight Loss

Kale and Kiwi Smoothie

Serves: 2

Prep time: 2-3 min

Ingredients:

2-3 ice cubes

1 cup orange juice

1 small pear, peeled and chopped

2 kiwi, peeled and chopped

2-3 kale leaves

2-3 dates, pitted

Directions:

Combine all ingredients in a high speed blender and blend until smooth.

Delicious Broccoli Smoothie

Serves: 2

Prep time: 2-3 min

Ingredients:

2-3 frozen broccoli florets

1 cup coconut milk

1 banana, peeled and chopped

1 cup pineapple, cut

1 peach, chopped

1 tsp cinnamon

Directions:

Combine all ingredients in a high speed blender and blend until smooth.

Papaya Smoothie

Serves: 2

Prep time: 2-3 min

Ingredients:

2-3 frozen broccoli florets

1 cup orange juice

1 small ripe avocado, peeled, cored and diced

1 cup papaya

1 cup fresh strawberries

Directions:

Combine all ingredients in a high speed blender and blend until smooth.

Beet and Papaya Smoothie

Serves: 2

Prep time: 2-3 min

Ingredients:

3-4 ice cubes

1 cup orange juice

1 banana, peeled and chopped

1 cup papaya

1 small beet, peeled and cut

Directions:

Combine all ingredients in a high speed blender and blend until smooth.

Lean Green Smoothie

Serves: 2

Prep time: 2-3 min

Ingredients:

1 frozen banana, chopped

1 cup orange juice

2-3 kale leaves, stems removed

1 small cucumber, peeled and chopped

1/2 cup fresh parsley leaves

½ tsp grated ginger

Directions:

Combine all ingredients in a high speed blender and blend until smooth.

Easy Antioxidant Smoothie

Serves: 2

Prep time: 2-3 min

Ingredients:

2-3 frozen broccoli florets

1 cup orange juice

2 plums, cut

1 cup raspberries

1 tsp ginger powder

Directions:

Combine all ingredients in a high speed blender and blend until smooth.

Healthy Purple Smoothie

Serves: 2

Prep time: 2-3 min

Ingredients:

2-3 frozen broccoli florets

1 cup water

1/2 avocado, peeled and chopped

3 plums, chopped

1 cup blueberries

Directions:

Combine all ingredients in a high speed blender and blend until smooth.

Mom's Favorite Kale Smoothie

Serves: 2

Prep time: 2-3 min

Ingredients:

2-3 ice cubes

1½ cup orange juice

1 green small apple, cut

½ cucumber, chopped

2-3 leaves kale

½ cup raspberries

Directions:

Combine all ingredients in a high speed blender and blend until smooth.

Creamy Green Smoothie

Serves: 2

Prep time: 2-3 min

Ingredients:

1 frozen banana

1 cup coconut milk

1 small pear, chopped

1 cup baby spinach

1 cup grapes

1 tbsp coconut butter

1 tsp vanilla extract

Directions:

Combine all ingredients in a high speed blender and blend until smooth.

Strawberry and Arugula Smoothie

Serves: 2

Prep time: 2-3 min

Ingredients:

2 cups frozen strawberries

1 cup unsweetened almond milk

10-12 arugula leaves

1/2 tsp ground cinnamon

Directions:

Combine ice, almond milk, strawberries, arugula and cinnamon in a high speed blender. Blend until smooth and serve.

Emma's Amazing Smoothie

Serves: 2

Prep time: 2-3 min

Ingredients:

1 frozen banana, chopped

1 cup orange juice

1 large nectarine, sliced

1/2 zucchini, peeled and chopped

2-3 dates, pitted

Directions:

Combine all ingredients in a high speed blender and blend until smooth.

Good-To-Go Morning Smoothie

Serves: 2

Prep time: 2-3 min

Ingredients:

1 cup frozen strawberries

1 cup apple juice

1 banana, chopped

1 cup raw asparagus, chopped

1 tbsp ground flaxseed

Directions:

Combine all ingredients in a high speed blender and blend until smooth.

Endless Energy Smoothie

Serves: 2

Prep time: 2-3 min

Ingredients:

1 frozen banana, chopped

1 1/2 cup green tea

1 cup chopped pineapple

2 raw asparagus spears, chopped

1 lime, juiced

1 tbsp chia seeds

Directions:

Combine all ingredients in a high speed blender and blend until smooth.

High-fibre Fruit Smoothie

Serves: 2

Prep time: 2-3 min

Ingredients:

1 frozen banana, chopped

1 cup orange juice

2 cups chopped papaya

1 cup shredded cabbage

1 tbsp chia seeds

Directions:

Combine all ingredients in a high speed blender and blend until smooth.

Nutritious Green Smoothie

Serves: 2

Prep time: 2-3 min

Ingredients:

2-3 frozen broccoli florets

1 cup apple juice

1 large pear, chopped

1 kiwi, peeled and chopped

1 cup spinach leaves

1-2 dates, pitted

Directions:

Combine all ingredients in a high speed blender and blend until smooth.

Apricot, Strawberry and Banana Smoothie

Serves: 2

Prep time: 2-3 min

Ingredients:

1 frozen banana

1 1/2 cup almond milk

5 dried apricots

1 cup fresh strawberries

Directions:

Combine all ingredients in a high speed blender and blend until smooth.

Spinach and Green Apple Smoothie

Serves: 2

Prep time: 2-3 min

Ingredients:

3-4 ice cubes

1 cup unsweetened almond milk

1 banana, peeled and chopped

2 green apples, peeled and chopped

1 cup raw spinach leaves

3-4 dates, pitted

1 tsp grated ginger

Directions:

Combine all ingredients in a high speed blender and blend until smooth.

Superfood Blueberry Smoothie

Serves: 2

Prep time: 2-3 min

Ingredients:

2-3 cubes frozen spinach

1 cup green tea

1 banana

2 cups blueberries

1 tbsp ground flaxseed

Directions:

Combine all ingredients in a high speed blender and blend until smooth.

Zucchini and Blueberry Smoothie

Serves: 2

Prep time: 2-3 min

Ingredients:

1 cup frozen blueberries

1 cup unsweetened almond milk

1 banana

1 zucchini, peeled and chopped

Directions:

Combine all ingredients in a high speed blender and blend until smooth.

Tropical Spinach Smoothie

Serves: 2

Prep time: 2-3 min

Ingredients:

1/2 cup crushed ice or 3-4 ice cubes

1 cup coconut milk

1 mango, peeled and diced

1 cup fresh spinach leaves

4-5 dates, pitted

1/2 tsp vanilla extract

Directions:

Combine all ingredients in a high speed blender and blend until smooth.

Dark Green Veggie Smoothie

Serves: 2

Prep time: 2-3 min

Ingredients:

3-4 frozen spinach cubes

1 cup water

1 cup chopped kale, trimmed, chopped, tightly packed

1 banana, chopped

1 large apple chopped

1 pear, chopped

Directions:

Combine all ingredients in a high speed blender and blend until smooth.

Kale and Raspberry Smoothie

Serves: 2

Prep time: 2-3 min

Ingredients:

2-3 ice cubes

1 cup almond milk

1/2 avocado, pitted, peeled and chopped

3-4 kale leaves

2 cups raspberries

Directions:

Combine all ingredients in a high speed blender and blend until smooth.

Delicious Kale Smoothie

Serves: 2

Prep time: 2-3 min

Ingredients:

2-3 ice cubes

1 1/2 cups apple juice

3-4 kale leaves

2 figs, chopped

1 cup strawberries

Directions:

Combine all ingredients in a high speed blender and blend until smooth.

Healthy Apricot Smoothie

Serves: 2

Prep time: 2-3 min

Ingredients:

2-3 ice cubes

1 cup almond milk

1/2 avocado, peeled and chopped

4 apricots, chopped

1 apple, chopped

5-6 arugula leaves

Directions:

Combine all ingredients in a high speed blender and blend until smooth.

Cherry Smoothie

Serves: 2

Prep time: 2-3 min

Ingredients:

1 frozen banana, chopped

1 cup almond milk

2 cups pitted cherries

1 tsp cinnamon

Directions :

Combine all ingredients in a high speed blender and blend until smooth.

About the Author

Alissa Grey is a fitness and nutrition enthusiast that loves to teach people about losing weight and feeling better about themselves. She lives in a small French village in the foothills of a beautiful mountain range with her husband, three teenage kids, two free spirited dogs, and various other animals.

Alissa Grey is incredibly lucky to be able to cook and eat natural foods, mostly grown nearby, something she's done since she was a teenager. She enjoys yoga, running, reading, hanging out with her family, and growing organic vegetables and herbs.

Printed in Great Britain
by Amazon